EL CHINO

ALLEN SAY

Houghton Mifflin Company Boston 1990

Library of Congress Cataloging-in-Publication Data

Say, Allen.
   El Chino / Allen Say.
      p.   cm.
      Summary: A biography of Bill Wong, a Chinese American who became a
   famous bullfighter in Spain.
      ISBN 0-395-52023-1
      1. El Chino (Bong Way Wong)—Juvenile literature.
   2. Bullfighters—United States—Biography—Juvenile literature.
   [1. El Chino (Bong Way Wong) 2. Bullfighters.] I. Title.
   GV1108.E5S39   1990   90-35026
   791.8′2′092—dc20   CIP
   [B]   AC
   [92]

Printed in the United States of America
HOR 10 9 8 7 6 5 4 3 2 1

This book is dedicated to the brothers
and sisters of Bill Wong: Lily, Rose, Jack,
Florence, and Art. And my special thanks to
Janet, who first told me about Bill.

— A.S.

My parents came from Canton, China, and had six children in Nogales, Arizona. I was the fourth child. They named me Bong Way Wong, but my brothers and sisters called me Billy.

Our home was a corner grocery store, and we were open
for business every day of the year.

"In America, you can be anything you want to be," Dad told us.

That was good news because none of us wanted to be a grocer
when we grew up.

Lily, the eldest, was studying to be a librarian. Rose and Florence wanted to be teachers. My older brother, Jack, loved engineering. And Art, my baby brother, said he was going to be a doctor.

All I wanted to do was play basketball.

"Who's ever heard of a Chinese athlete!" They laughed.

They didn't understand. I wanted to be a *great* athlete.

"Why don't you listen to Dad," I told them.

But Dad died suddenly when I was ten. Our days were dark
after that, and we had to be a stronger family than we were
before. We gathered around Mom and went on with our business.

In high school I finally got to play serious basketball.
I was quick and fast, and I could shoot from
anywhere on the court. "My ace," the coach used to call me.
But I never got to play in college. I was too short.

"Just think," I said to my brother, Jack. "Four inches taller and I would've been famous!"

"Who's going to hire a Chinese ballplayer, anyway?" he asked. "Learn a trade and earn a living like everybody else."

So, like Jack, I studied engineering.

After college I got a job as a highway engineer. That made everybody happy, especially Mom.

But I kept thinking about shooting the winning basket with the clock running out.

"Give Billy the ball!" they used to yell.

And they always did. I'd spin and shoot all in one motion, and the whole gym would explode with my name.

"Billy! Billy! Billy!"

I never forgot that.

Give me the ball!

But by then I had a trade and earned a living. For my first
vacation I went to Europe. I liked Spain best —
it was hot there, like it was in Arizona. I saw castles and
museums, cathedrals and Gypsy dancers.

Then I saw a bullfight.

It's a sport where the bullfighter fools the bull with a cloth cape and kills it with a sword. Sometimes the bull kills the bullfighter. It wasn't anything like the rodeo shows I'd seen back home.

The first time the bull charged the bullfighter, I closed
my eyes.

"Olé!" The crowd screamed, and I paid attention.

It was a spectacle, all right, a very dangerous circus.
And the bullfighter was some kind of an athlete. He was graceful,
too, like a ballet dancer, and had the steadiest nerves I'd ever
seen. The bull kept missing him, and with each miss the audience
yelled louder. I shouted with them, until my voice was gone.

When the fight was over, the bull was dead. And now it
was the people who charged the bullfighter. Roaring at the
top of their voices, they hoisted him onto their shoulders
and marched out of the arena. I rushed after them.

I didn't have to chase far. I even managed to stand
right next to the amazing daredevil, and I got a shock. He was
much shorter than me!

That night I didn't sleep. I couldn't get him to stop
dancing inside my head, that short Spaniard in a fancy
outfit.

In the morning, I bought myself some Spanish clothes.
Then I got a room in a boarding house, where I put away my
old clothes and put on the new. In the mirror, I looked like
a fine Spanish gentleman.

Using my hands and arms, I asked the landlady, "Where
is the bullfighting school?"

"Ah, Señor." She gazed at me with great pity in her eyes.
"Only the Spaniards can become true matadors."

She sounded like my mother. And that reminded me to
send Mom a telegram, and also one to my boss. Very sorry and
please forgive, I am not coming home.

The school was just a clearing in a wood outside the city,
but the maestro had been a famous matador when he was young.
We took turns playing the bull, and the old master taught us
to use the cape and the sword.

"He is a good athlete," I heard one student say about me.

"And he has courage and grace," said another. "But he cannot be a matador. He is not Spanish."

My dad would've said a few things to them, but it was no use. How could they understand? They hadn't grown up in the United States.

Before I knew, it was springtime in Spain. That's when the bull ranchers hired student matadors to test their young cows for courage and spirit. And the students who fought well would go on to become real matadors. Like my classmates, I went looking for work.

Everywhere I went, though, the ranchers took one look at me and shook their heads. My family sent me love and money, and that kept me going, but after two years I still hadn't fought a single cow. Maybe it was time to give up, time to go home and be an engineer again.

But what would Dad have said to me now?

I'd tell him this wasn't Arizona, U.S.A. So I couldn't be a Spanish matador.

But *uno momento*, Señor. A Spanish matador? What had I been thinking all this time?

I'm Chinese!

I searched all over town, and finally found what I was looking for — a Chinese costume. I tried it on and hardly recognized myself in the mirror.

It was as if I were seeing myself for the first time. I looked like a *real* Chinese. And as I stared in the mirror, a strange feeling came over me. I felt powerful. I felt that I could do anything I wished — even become a matador! Could it be that I was wearing a magical costume?

I went outside to see what would happen.

I was a spectacle.

Children followed me everywhere I went. Men greeted me
from across the street. Women smiled.

"El Chino!" they shouted. The Chinese!

For the first time, people were taking notice of me,
and that was magic.

It was time to go see a bull rancher.

Sure enough, the first rancher I saw gave me the nod.
Just like that, I was facing my first live bull.
　　Actually, it was only a heifer, but it looked more
like a black rhino, with horns that could gore right through me.

"I will not back off," I said to myself, and waved the cape. The black hulk stood still, swishing a tail like a lion's.

"*Ojo, toro-o-o!*" I called, giving the cape a good flap.

The charge was sudden and fast.

Like a tumbling boulder, the heifer came straight at me, and I swung the cape. At the last moment she swerved and went for the cape. *Swoosh!* With a hot wind she was past me. I spun around, flapped the cape, and she charged again. Then again.

I didn't remember how many passes I'd made before I heard the ranch hands shouting. They wanted to see how I would end the fight.

So I made her charge me one more time, and then I walked away without looking back, as I had seen real matadors do. I prayed the heifer wouldn't gore me in my back. She didn't move.

"Olé, olé!" The crowd applauded me. I'd passed the test.

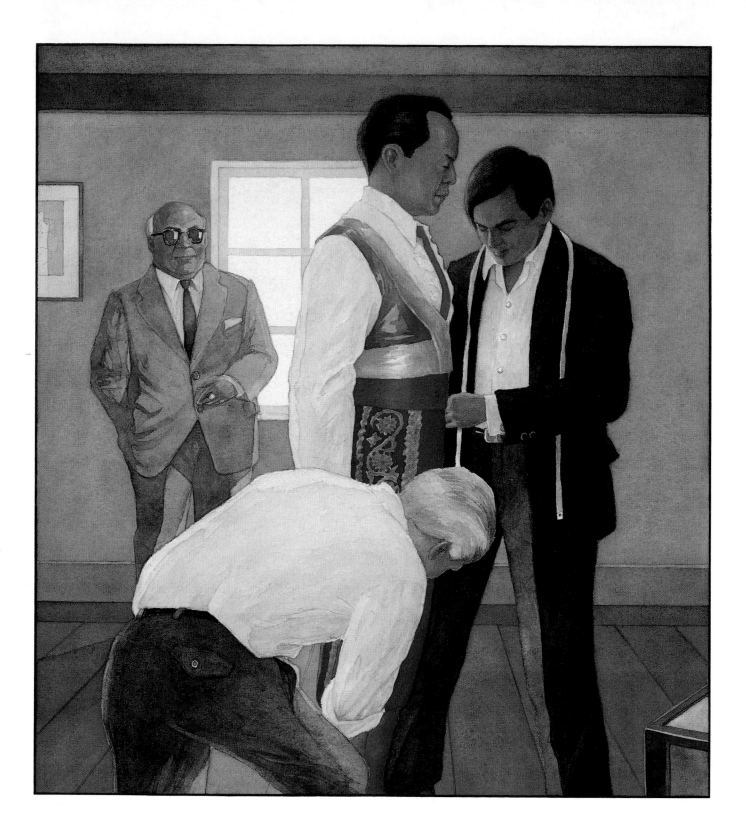

The next morning a bald-headed man came knocking on my door.

"I hear good things about you, Señor," he said. "I am a manager of bullfighters. Do you want me to help you become a matador?"

"Sí!" I almost shouted. "I would be honored!"

"*Bueno*. But you cannot fight in your strange costume. Come with me," he said, and took me to a tailor's shop.

There, I was fitted for the "suit of lights," which all matadors wear in bullrings. I felt like a prince being groomed for an important ceremony.

And there *was* a ceremony. My manager had made an arrangement for me to fight a real bull in a month's time!

"You are a sensation," he told me. "The plaza is sold out, and it is El Chino everyone wants to see."

Finally it was my day.

In a short while my manager would be arriving with a lot of reporters and photographers. I was big news. And my manager was supposed to help me get into the "suit of lights," but I couldn't wait any longer and got into it on my own.

In the mirror I looked splendid.

"Good thing you weren't four inches taller," I said to myself. "Show them you have grace and courage like the best of them. Don't lose face, for your family's sake . . ."

As I stared in the mirror, I began to feel victorious already. There had never been a Chinese matador before me. I could almost hear the sold-out plaza cheering me on. And if I fought well, maybe a crowd of Spaniards would carry me out of the arena on their shoulders, shouting my name the whole time.

And that's the way it happened. Just as I had dreamed it.
"Olé! El Chino, olé!"